T0394855

THE CUBAN MISSILE CRISIS

Nick Rebman

Apex is distributed by North Star Editions:
sales@northstareditions.com | 888-417-0195

Produced for Apex by Red Line Editorial.

Photographs ©: Robert Knudsen/White House Photographs/John F. Kennedy Presidential Library and Museum, cover, 1, 30–31; Martin Brown/National Archives, 4–5; Shutterstock Images, 6–7, 10–11; JFK Presidential Library and Museum/National Archives/DVIDS, 8–9; Library of Congress, 12–13; Corbis Historical/Getty Images, 14–15; Hulton Archive/Archive Photos/Getty Images, 16–17; Joe Davila/US Air Force, 19; Warren K. Leffler/Library of Congress, 20–21; US Air Force, 22–23, 28–29, 44–45, 58; Keystone-France/Gamma-Keystone/Getty Images, 24–25, 32–33, 38–39; Bettmann/Getty Images, 26–27, 42–43; AP Images, 34–35; National Archives/Naval History and Heritage Command, 36–37, 46–47; Archivio GBB/Alamy, 41; Getty Images News/Getty Images, 48–49; Ron Case/Hulton Archive/Getty Images, 50–51; Charles Tasnadi/AP Images, 52–53; Stephen Jaffe/Hulton Archive/Getty Images, 54–55; Lt. Cmdr. Michael L. Smith/US Navy, 56–57

Library of Congress Control Number: 2024943629

ISBN
979-8-89250-463-8 (hardcover)
979-8-89250-479-9 (paperback)
979-8-89250-509-3 (ebook pdf)
979-8-89250-495-9 (hosted ebook)

Printed in the United States of America
Mankato, MN
012025

NOTE TO PARENTS AND EDUCATORS

Apex books are designed to build literacy skills in striving readers. Exciting, high-interest content attracts and holds readers' attention. The text is carefully leveled to allow students to achieve success quickly.

TABLE OF CONTENTS

Chapter 1

SPY PLANE

An American pilot climbed into his plane. He took off from California. He was flying a U-2 spy plane. The date was October 14, 1962. The pilot had a long flight ahead. He had an important job to do.

The first U-2 planes took flight in 1955. The US military was still using them in the 2020s.

Florida

Cuba is less than 100 miles (160 km) from the US coast.

Cuba

The pilot headed for Florida. But first, he flew over Cuba. The United States viewed Cuba as an enemy. So, the pilot was careful. He flew very high in the sky. That way, he would be safe. Enemy weapons could not reach him. The pilot took pictures of Cuba. Then he landed in Florida.

MRBM FIELD LAUNCH SITE
SAN CRISTOBAL NO 1
14 OCTOBER 1962

The spy plane's photos showed many weapons in Cuba.

ERECTOR LAUNCHER EQUIPMENT

ERECTOR LAUNCHER EQUIPMENT

8 MISSILE TRAILERS

EQUIPMENT

TENT AREAS

Military experts looked at the photos. They saw nuclear missiles. The Soviet Union had put those missiles in Cuba. The photos also showed launch sites. These sites could send out missiles. They could hit the United States. US leaders feared an attack.

NUCLEAR WEAPONS

Nuclear weapons are very powerful. They release huge amounts of energy. They create very high temperatures. Their blasts are hotter than the sun. Even one nuclear bomb can destroy a whole city. Many people can be hurt or killed.

Approximately 200,000 people died in the nuclear bombings of Japan.

Chapter 2

THE COLD WAR

Nuclear bombs were first used in World War II (1939–1945). Many countries were involved in the war. The United States and Soviet Union were allies. In August 1945, US planes dropped two nuclear bombs on Japan. The war ended soon after.

After World War II, Harry S. Truman (center) led the United States. Joseph Stalin (right) led the Soviet Union.

Things changed quickly after the war. The United States and the Soviet Union became enemies. They disagreed about big ideas. One was how governments should be run. Another was how economies should work. The United States supported capitalism. The Soviet Union supported Communism.

TAKING SIDES

Countries took sides after World War II. The United States was part of NATO. This group included most of Western Europe. NATO supported capitalism. The Soviet Union formed the Warsaw Pact. This group included most of Eastern Europe. It supported Communism.

The conflict became known as the Cold War (1947–1991). The United States built many nuclear bombs. The Soviet Union did as well. Both sides tested their bombs. The bombs became more and more powerful.

OTHER WARS

US and Soviet troops did not fight each other directly. But they helped in several wars. And they backed different sides. One example was the Korean War (1950–1953). The United States helped South Korea. The Soviet Union helped North Korea.

Countries have carried out more than 2,000 nuclear tests since 1945.

The Cold War was a scary time. People worried that a nuclear war would start. This threat rose in the 1950s. New missiles were a main reason. The missiles could carry nuclear bombs. The Soviet Union had built them by 1958. The United States had them the next year. The missiles were very fast. And they could travel far. They could start a nuclear war.

Missiles could fly nuclear weapons across oceans.

DANGERS OF WAR

The United States and the Soviet Union were both ready to use their nuclear weapons. But if one country attacked, the other country would strike back. Planes, submarines, and missiles would all attack with nuclear bombs.

> **By 1960, both sides had enough nuclear weapons to end all life on Earth.**

This would be a nuclear war. No one would win. Both countries would be destroyed. Millions of people would die on each side.

US and Soviet leaders both knew of this danger. Neither side wanted to use its weapons. But each wanted to have them as a warning.

Chapter 3

CHANGE COMES TO CUBA

In 1959, Cuba changed leaders. Communist forces took control. Fidel Castro became the leader. Cuba is an island that is close to the US coast. So, these changes worried US leaders.

Fidel Castro's rise to power was called the Cuban Revolution.

21

US leaders did not want Communism to expand. So, they didn't like Cuba's new leader. They also worried that nearby countries might turn to Communism. US leaders decided to take action. They made plans to kill Castro. They hoped to end Communism in Cuba.

MANY MISSILES

US leaders tried to stop Communism in many ways. They often focused on the Soviet Union. In 1959, the United States put some nuclear weapons in Turkey. This country was near the Soviet Union. So, the missiles could quickly reach Soviet targets.

The US military tests a Jupiter missile in 1959. The United States stored Jupiter missiles in Turkey.

The United States trained a small army. It was made up of anti-Communist Cubans. In April 1961, this army acted. The fighters tried to take over Cuba. But the invasion failed. Cuban forces won easily. The event became known as the Bay of Pigs invasion.

Cuba defeated more than 1,000 US-trained forces during the Bay of Pigs invasion.

TRAINING TERRORISTS

When Castro took power, many Cubans left. Many went to the United States. The United States trained some of them. These Cubans formed the small army. They learned how to use terrorism. US leaders thought these actions could help take down Castro.

Nikita Khrushchev took over the Soviet Union after Joseph Stalin died in 1953.

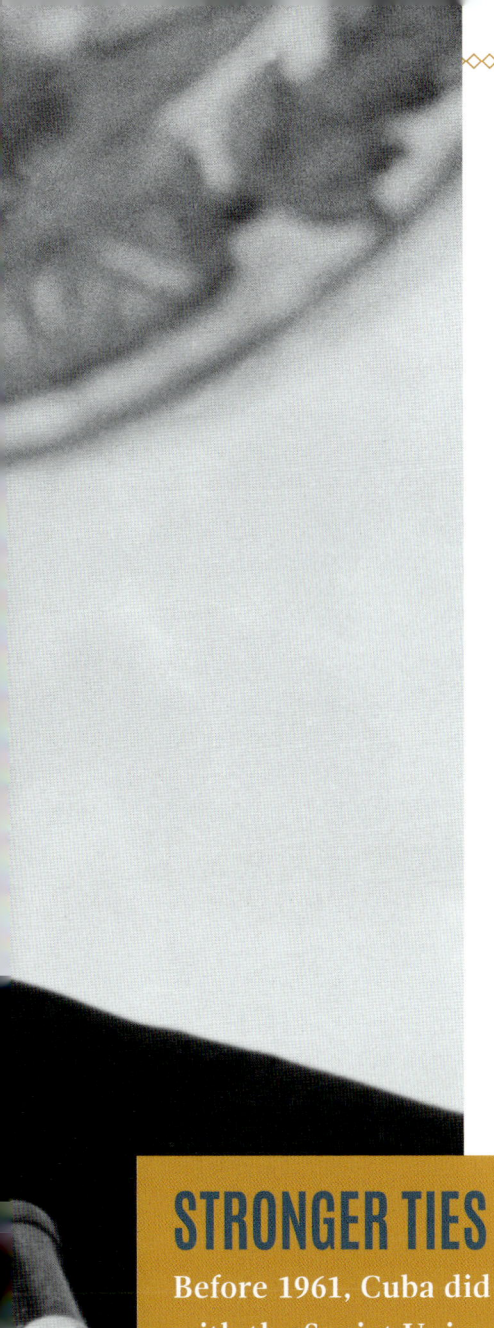

In 1961, Nikita Khrushchev led the Soviet Union. He was angry about the Bay of Pigs invasion. He did not want the United States to try again. In July 1962, Khrushchev talked to Castro. They came up with a secret plan. The Soviet Union would help Cuba. It would send nuclear missiles to the island.

STRONGER TIES

Before 1961, Cuba did not have strong ties with the Soviet Union. That changed after the Bay of Pigs invasion. The Soviet Union started helping Cuba more. Many Soviet soldiers went to the island. They guarded the missiles.

A US spy plane spotted the missiles on October 14, 1962. The US government knew that Soviet weapons could now reach much of the United States.

President John F. Kennedy thought about his options. He could bomb Cuba from the air. He could invade from the ground. Or US ships could put a blockade around Cuba. That way, Soviet ships could not reach the island.

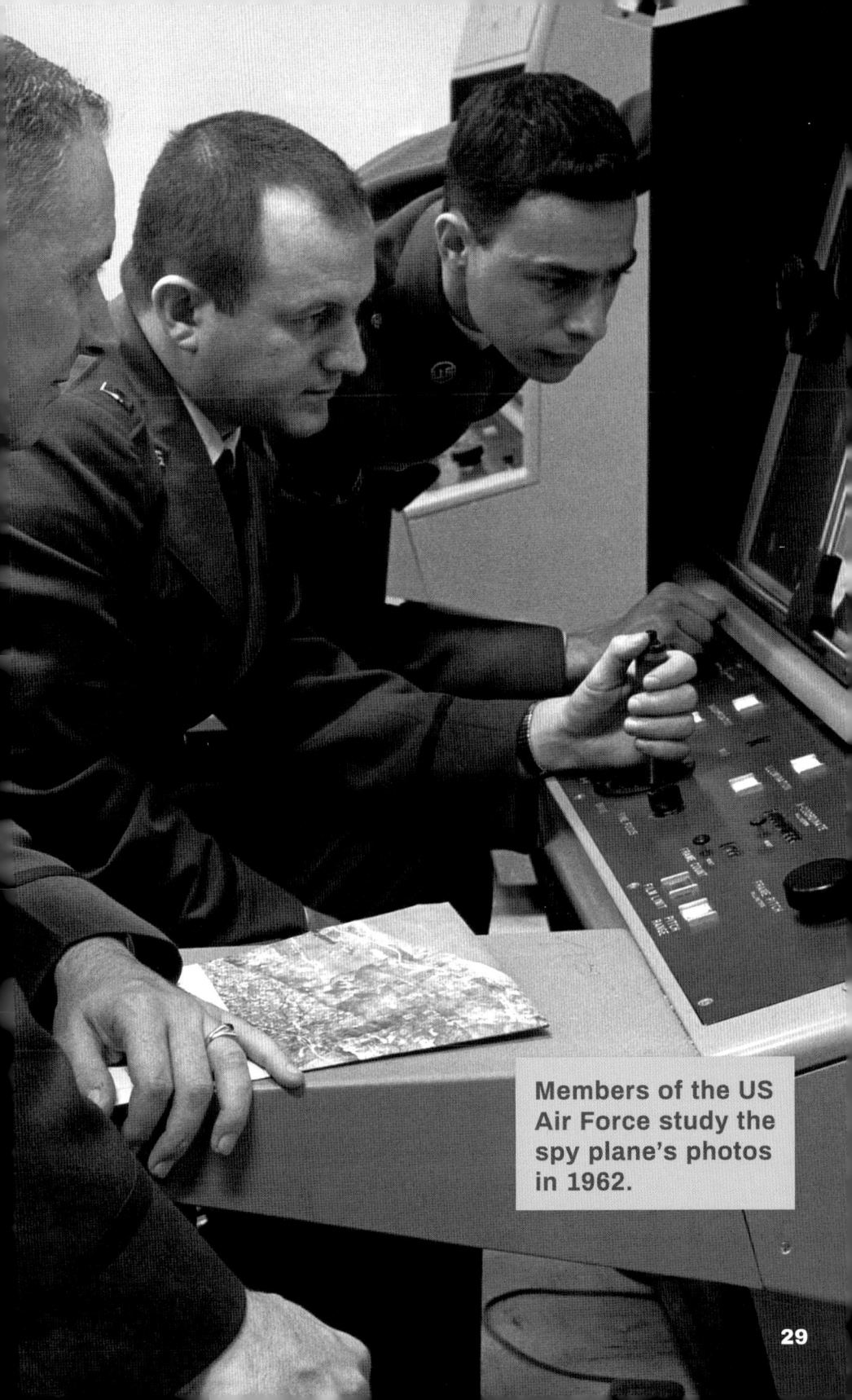

Members of the US Air Force study the spy plane's photos in 1962.

Chapter 4

ON THE BRINK

On October 22, 1962, Kennedy spoke on TV. He talked about the Soviet Union. He said the country had put nuclear missiles in Cuba. Kennedy also sent US ships toward Cuba. These ships would not let Soviet ships near the island. That way, more missiles could not enter Cuba.

President John F. Kennedy gave his speech from the Oval Office of the White House.

On October 23, several Soviet ships stopped at sea. They did not try to enter Cuba. But the crisis wasn't over. Soviet soldiers were still in Cuba. And they were building launch sites. Many people worried. They feared a nuclear war would soon begin.

US ships patrol waters near Cuba on October 23, 1962.

SUBMARINES

The Soviets had submarines. By October 23, several subs were near Cuba. They had gone there in secret. And they stayed underwater. That way, they would be harder to spot. These subs carried nuclear weapons.

Khrushchev was angry. On October 24, he sent Kennedy a message. He talked about the Soviet ships. He said they had the right to enter Cuba. And he would not tell the ships to turn around.

AGAINST THE LAW

Laws tell countries how they can treat one another. Some actions are not allowed. One is blocking supplies to another country. That's against the law during peace. Khrushchev told Kennedy this.

The crisis in Cuba alarmed the world. Leaders of many countries argued about it on October 25.

UNITED ARAB REPUBLIC

UNITED KINGDOM

By October 26, danger was near. US forces were on high alert. They had several plans. One was launching a nuclear attack on Cuba. Another was invading the island. Kennedy leaned toward invading. He wanted to get rid of the Soviet missiles. He thought this was the only way.

A DANGEROUS ASK

Castro sent Khrushchev a message on October 26. Castro thought the United States would invade soon. He asked for help if that happened. He wanted the Soviet Union to attack the United States. Castro wanted to start a nuclear war. Khrushchev said that was too dangerous.

On October 26, crew members from a US destroyer (left) stopped and inspected a Soviet ship (right).

The next day was a turning point. Cuba's missiles were ready to launch. And that wasn't all. A US spy plane flew over Cuba. Soviet soldiers saw it. They shot it down. The pilot died. US military leaders wanted to attack Cuba. But Kennedy waited. US and Soviet leaders were still negotiating. They looked for a way to end the crisis.

The US spy plane was shot down on October 27. The plane crashed in Cuba.

VASILI ARKHIPOV

Vasili Arkhipov worked on a Soviet submarine. He was one of three officers on board. On October 27, a US ship spotted this sub. It tried to force the submarine to the surface.

The Soviet officers had to respond. The other two wanted to attack the US ship. That attack would have started a nuclear war. However, all three officers had to agree. And Arkhipov refused. So, the submarine went to the surface. Arkhipov had prevented war.

Few people knew about Vasili Arkhipov's actions until after his death in 1998.

The US military built up defenses on the Florida coast during the crisis.

The crisis entered day 13 on October 28. Finally, a deal was reached. Both sides agreed to key things. Khrushchev would remove the missiles from Cuba. Soviet radio announced this decision. That way, the deal would be made public.

In return, Kennedy would not attack Cuba. This was also made public. People around the world felt great relief. The crisis was over at last. The two sides had avoided a nuclear war.

US leaders showed photos to the public to prove that missiles were leaving Cuba.

FORMER LAUNCH POSITIONS

MRBM LAUNCH SITE 2
SAN CRISTOBAL

FUEL TRAILERS

RMER LOCATION OF MISSILE-READY TENTS

45

The United States agreed to another action. It would remove its missiles from Turkey. But this part of the deal stayed secret. Only US and Soviet leaders knew. US leaders believed Turkey would be angry. Turkey would feel less safe without the missiles.

LOOKING WEAK

The secrecy caused problems for Khrushchev. People only knew about part of what he gained in the deal. So, they thought he backed down. This made him look weak.

The US military kept close watch on Cuban and Soviet forces after the crisis ended.

US and Soviet leaders talked only to one another. They did not include Castro. As a result, Castro felt very angry. He had wanted to play a bigger role. Cuba was also losing the missiles. So, Castro thought Cuba would become less safe.

NO INSPECTORS

Inspectors were another part of the deal. Cuba was supposed to let them in. They would make sure the missiles were being removed. But Castro refused. So, US leaders found another way. US planes flew above the Soviet ships. The pilots saw the missiles leaving Cuba.

A US plane flies above a Soviet ship to make sure it is removing nuclear missiles.

Chapter 6

LEGACY

US and Soviet leaders faced off in October 1962. Nuclear war nearly happened. The event became known as the Cuban Missile Crisis. During that time, Kennedy and Khrushchev had to send messages to talk. The messages took hours to arrive. The leaders wanted a faster way. So, they set up a line of direct communication. That let them call each other quickly on a secure line.

The Cuban Missile Crisis is one of the main events that Kennedy (left) and Khrushchev (right) are remembered for.

The United States kept its promise. It did not invade Cuba. However, US leaders were still against Castro. They made more secret plans. They tried to kill Castro. Nothing worked, though. Castro stayed in power for years. He stepped down in 2008.

CHANGING TIES

The Cuban Missile Crisis changed many things. It weakened Soviet ties with Cuba. This shift hurt Cuba's economy. But ties grew stronger in the late 1960s. The Soviet Union started giving Cuba more aid.

The United States tried to kill Fidel Castro in many ways. They even tried poisoning Castro's ice cream.

US-Soviet ties improved as the 1960s went on. The countries did not want another crisis. The two sides still didn't trust each other. But they were more careful. They talked about ways to keep the peace. Even so, the Cold War continued until 1991.

Berlin, Germany, was divided during the Cold War. In 1989, the Berlin Wall finally fell. The city became united again.

LOSING POWER

Khrushchev lost power in 1964. Other Soviet leaders thought he was weak. They did not like how he had handled the crisis. So, they forced him to step down.

The crisis also led to nuclear weapons deals. US and Soviet leaders signed one deal in 1963. It limited nuclear testing. Leaders signed another deal in 1968. It limited the number of bombs countries could make. However, nuclear weapons are still a threat. There are thousands in the world today.

In 2024, 14 US submarines carried nuclear weapons around the world. So did 31 submarines from other countries.

TIMELINE

JANUARY 1959	Communist forces led by Fidel Castro take control of Cuba.
APRIL 1961	The United States backs an invasion of Cuba, but the invasion fails. It becomes known as the Bay of Pigs invasion.
JULY 1962	The Soviet Union agrees to send nuclear missiles to Cuba to help prevent a US invasion.
OCTOBER 14, 1962	A US spy plane takes pictures of the Soviet missiles in Cuba.
OCTOBER 22, 1962	US president John F. Kennedy says US ships will block Cuba. That way, more Soviet weapons cannot enter the country.
OCTOBER 26, 1962	US forces get ready to invade Cuba.
OCTOBER 27, 1962	Soviet soldiers shoot down a US spy plane over Cuba.
OCTOBER 28, 1962	The United States agrees not to invade Cuba. The Soviet Union agrees to remove its missiles.

COMPREHENSION QUESTIONS

Write your answers on a separate piece of paper.

1. Write a paragraph that explains the main ideas of Chapter 3.

2. Do you think the United States should have supported the Bay of Pigs invasion? Why or why not?

3. When did Nikita Khrushchev lose power?

   A. 1962
   B. 1964
   C. 1968

4. What was most likely to happen if US forces had invaded Cuba in October 1962?

   A. The Soviet Union would have left Cuba right away.
   B. A nuclear war would have started, killing millions.
   C. The Soviet Union would have sided with US forces.

5. What does **targets** mean in this book?

*This country was near the Soviet Union. So, the missiles could quickly reach Soviet **targets**.*

    A. things that people plan to attack

    B. ways of talking to one another

    C. offers to reach peace

6. What does **negotiating** mean in this book?

*US and Soviet leaders were still **negotiating**. They looked for a way to end the crisis.*

    A. taking control of a country

    B. trying to solve a problem

    C. trying to start a war

Answer key on page 64.

GLOSSARY

allies
People or countries that agree to work together.

blockade
When an area is closed off so nothing can go in or out.

capitalism
A system in which people own property and work to make money.

Communism
An idea that calls for all property to be owned by the public.

crisis
A time of great danger or serious problems.

economies
Systems of goods, services, money, and jobs.

expand
To become more common.

inspectors
People who check something to make sure it is acceptable.

invasion
The act of entering a country in order to take over.

missiles
Weapons that are fired or launched at a target.

terrorism
The use of violence to scare others in order to reach a goal.

TO LEARN MORE

BOOKS

Boutland, Craig. *What Happened During the Cuban Missile Crisis?* New York: Rosen Publishing, 2024.

Huddleston, Emma. *How the Bomb Changed Everything.* Minneapolis: Abdo Publishing, 2022.

Stratton, Connor. *The Cold War.* Mendota Heights, MN: Focus Readers, 2024.

ONLINE RESOURCES

Visit **www.apexeditions.com** to find links and resources related to this title.

ABOUT THE AUTHOR

Nick Rebman is a writer and editor who lives in Minnesota.

INDEX

ANSWER KEY:

1. Answers will vary; 2. Answers will vary; 3. B; 4. B; 5. A; 6. B